Between Us Fathers

BETWEEN US FATHERS

LARRY LINK

BROADMAN PRESS
Nashville, Tennessee

© Copyright 1989 • Broadman Press
All Rights Reserved
4256-73

ISBN: 0-8054-5673-2
Dewey Decimal Classification:
Subject Heading:
Library of Congress Catalog Number: 88–7935

Printed in the United States of America

Library of Congress Cataloging-in-Publication Data

Link, Larry, 1942–
  Between us fathers / Larry Link.
    p.   cm.
  ISBN 0–8054–5673–2
  1. Fathers.   I. Title.
HQ756.L54   1989
306.8'742—dc19   88–7935
                                                         CIP

To my inspirations, my family:
LaVon, my wife;
My children—
Jarrod,
Josh, and
Katy

Contents

1
Who's Number One?

During a Sunday morning church service, my wife LaVon felt a nudge from our daughter Katy. This was not unusual, of course, so she responded. When she looked at Katy, she was handed a note—again, nothing unusual. The contents of the note, at first glance, would be hilarious—then, on second and third glances would be rather jolting. . . .

Dear Mom,
   Which of these men do you like best?
   (1) Robert Redford
   (2) Tom Cruise
   (3) Jesus

What would you do? How would your wife answer? How would your children respond to the questionnaire? This experience has been fun to relate, but the haunting question of the incident has been, "Katy surely does know the importance of Jesus in our lives—doesn't she, or does she?" We talk plenty about church and church activities, about Bible classes and worship, choir and children or youth meetings, but how much time do we spend talking about Jesus? (By the way, did you notice that *I* didn't even make "the list"?) The point of all this is for us to look more closely at how our values are translated to our children.

The last few weeks before Jarrod and Josh (our sons) left for college this summer, I had this overwhelming urge to give them a crash course on "Values 101" ("Just in case you missed this lesson somewhere along the way, let's cover it now.") So, I felt compelled to go through A—Z/Alpha—Omega, a remedial short course in "What to do if . . . " while away at school. Finally, I stopped and became rational. I asked myself, *Self, why have you—*

> —*brought your children up in church?*
> —*set aside hundreds of family nights in their grow-ing-up years?*
> —*had hundreds of breakfasts with them?*
> —*been involved in their church, school, and athletic activities?*
> —*opened our home to their friends?*
> —*talked with them about the Lord, our family, their decisions, their future, who they are, and whose they are, plus a myriad of other topics that all parents go through with their children?*

Why did I feel compelled to talk to them again, and why was Katy's note a hilarious/alarming note? Because we, as parents, find it so difficult to trust our offspring with making mature choices. Our responsibility is to create the environment for healthy decisions to be made. The question comes back—*How?* I'm glad you asked.

In our Sunday evening sessions at church which

we've had on " Parenting: Privilege and Responsibility," it's easy to see that when the " responsibilities" have been taken care of, the "privileges" will become more apparent. Many "ingredients" will make the environment a healthy one to give your children a sense of confidence in themselves (which is one of the most important factors in making right choices). Children *will* feel a sense of belonging when they have the following in their home:

- Quality time given to them by their parents (that's plural, Dad)
- Fun activities (fun to *them*)
- A comfortable, " warm" home (has nothing to do with the thermostat)
- A sense of family pride-identity (*only* happens when you do things together)
- A family that thinks "we" (concern for the other family members—no room for the Looking-out-for-Number-One philosophy)
- An assumption that church and spiritual matters have priority (and that priority should have its *primary* emphasis at home)

I can assure you that there will *still* be some wrong choices made—that's inevitable. But you will have done about all you can do.

At this "midterm" time, what are your grades in each of these areas? How do you measure up? As we look at our children's report cards, it's easy for us to evaluate and give advice. If your family were to "evaluate" you in your leadership in each of these areas, what would their "advice" be? Set the stage, create the environment. Who is most important in your house . . .

Robert Redford?

Tom Cruise?

Jesus? ? ?

2
Broken Window Panes

On a recent Sunday afternoon, I relearned a valuable lesson in parenting—about when to get upset with your children, no matter what their ages!

It was one of those Sundays when I needed to be back at the church by 3:15 for a couple of meetings. I also had to study for a session I was leading that night at 5:45. It was right after Christmas, and I was determined to disassemble the outdoor Christmas lights. After lunch I began removing the lights, which took longer than I had planned. I put them away and thought I could "Brush up" on my notes for twenty or thirty minutes before going to church. It was now 2:40.

Jarrod and Josh had been watching a ball game, and it was still halftime. As I was sitting on the couch studying, I heard them say, " Let's go throw some passes." I responded, "Can't right now, guys. Gotta study."

Less than thirty seconds later I heard an "explosion" I hadn't heard for years. I knew immediately what it was. LaVon was working on one of her "projects" in the same room with me, and she thought one of our antique cabinets had fallen over because of the nature of the sound—broken glass. Josh had thrown a "bullet" that was a little high for Jarrod to catch, but it had been caught (not too neatly) by one of our dining room windows.

I didn't tell LaVon, Jarrod, or Josh, but I was inwardly grinning. I hadn't heard that sound in years! Not that I welcome someone breaking out our windows—I don't. But for only a fleeting moment Jarrod and Josh were ten and eleven years old again and sheepishly coming in to "face the music." We began cleaning up immediately and found glass everywhere—on the couch where I had been sitting and past the couch against a wall about thirty feet from the broken window pane. Needless to note, this threw a kink into my Sunday afternoon plans.

- No study time
- Hardware stores were closed—no window pane
- Makeshift window for the night
- Got to get to the church no later than 3:30
- "Whew!"

Reflection time later that night revealed a lot for me:

- *Larry, the first thing you need to remember is that both boys were home from college at the same time —pretty rare occurrence these days.*
- *You had your whole family in church today— equally as rare.*
- *If you hadn't been studying, you could have been the one throwing or trying to catch the pass.*
- *And, maybe most important, why would anyone let a broken window pane (which costs $1.81 to replace) upset them enough to cause a break in a relationship with his family?*

I had built a fire in our fireplace after church that night. As we were quietly sitting there later that evening, I caught myself staring into the fire as it burned lower and lower, and saying, "Thank You, Lord, for that broken window pane. It has reminded me again just how important my relationship is with my family."

Sometimes, Dads, we become upset over minor matters, so insignificant in the scope of eternity, or even in view of the brief eighteen-year (sometimes more) span when we have our children at home. Sometimes our expectations are so unrealistic that we jeopardize our relationship with our family over something that is so petty. How about it, Dad? What is really important enough to waste a good "mad" over? Are you losing your cool over things of little or no consequence?

Tonight, or even earlier, take inventory of the "broken windowpanes" of your household. Broken windowpanes don't need to cause broken relationships. Broken/damaged relationships for $1.81 and a little clean-up time? Hardly worth it.

3
Teamwork

"Way to go, Trey!" yelled the team and the crowd in the stands. He had stolen the ball, dribbled the length of the court, and made a basket. Trey was only a second grader and the youngest member of the coed basketball team I had been coaching at our church. My daughter, Katy, was on the team, and all the players in our league are either in the third or fourth grade, except a few like Trey who came in as second graders.

We had a fantastic time in those few weeks. Several of the kids didn't know how to dribble, pass, or shoot—and didn't know any of the rules, so we started from scratch. All of us learned along the way—including the coach! The kids became upset with each other sometimes, and they wildly cheered for one another when things were going well. They also helped each other when one or the other wasn't doing too well.

One of the fondest memories of the entire season, amid some very exciting games, happened, not at a Saturday-morning game or even a Tuesday-night practice. It occurred on Sunday morning when one of the girls on our team made a profession of faith in Christ. As a team, we talked about it the following Tuesday. It was a special time.

Through those weeks, the lesson I wanted all the kids to learn was about teamwork—and they did that. There are so many important things to learn from any sport, but the support and interdependence on one another is paramount. I had a flashback when Trey scored his bucket on his steal-back to my very first realization of what teamwork was all about . . .

I was living in Stillwater, Oklahoma, at the time. Stillwater was the home of Oklahoma A & M (now Oklahoma State University), and home of then-recent back-to-back national basketball titles under coach Henry "Fog Horn" Iba, also called the "Iron Duke of Basketball." Basketball fever had spread to every age in Stillwater, and I was no exception.

I was nine years old in 1951 when our basketball team was invited to play at halftime at an Oklahoma A & M game! Their field house, Gallagher Hall, seated about seven thousand, and it was literally packed for every game. That court looked like it was a mile long when we started our game, and we were used to playing to a crowd of twenty or thirty parents—not thousands of strangers!

I don't remember if we won or lost, but I'll never forget the lesson I learned in that game. My best friend Mickey stole the ball and passed it to me so I could take it the length of the court and score. I did—and the crowd went wild! Then, it hit me for the first time. In the middle of all that cheering for me, I looked at Mickey and he yelled, " Way to go!" *He* could have made that bucket, but he gave it to *me*. That's teamwork— what our coach had been trying to instill in us all season. I had finally learned it in the spotlight. I have replayed that lesson repeatedly because I feel strongly that teamwork must be a part of our lives every day at work and at home.

Teamwork at home is the most important place for all of us to learn what we must do to support, believe in, build up, draw from, and care for each other. What do you see when you look at any championship team? Every player knows his/her job and does it, while all the time they're *depending* on the others to do theirs.

How does all this basketball and teamwork stuff apply to you? Look at your family as a team, with the father in the role of player/coach. He is the person constantly involved in the life of that family, and, at the same time, is also helping, correcting, supporting, building up, encouraging, pulling the team together, disciplining, teaching—not from the bench, but out there on the court as a participant. We all know that the most effective way of teaching is "modeling." Whatever you want your children to become, you "model" for them. One of the most crucial aspects of "father-modeling," one that will have a profound influence on that child during childhood and adulthood and will greatly affect his relationship with his spouse, is how you treat your wife. How do you support, encourage, build up, and help your wife? Remember that on a team, everyone carries part of the load. Do you help carry the load? Do you help take care of the children? Do you help around the house? Why not? It's a team effort, remember? We expect our children to do certain chores around the house. Why not us dads? It's all about teamwork, modeling, and being a player/coach.

How are you at supporting? You have a prime opportunity to support, build up, encourage, and model as you truly show your wife how much you care not only on Valentine's Day but all during the year. Do something special! It doesn't have to be expensive; it simply needs to be an outward expression of support and love for your wife. You'll be a hero to your wife, a teacher to your children, and a much richer person for it.

The apostle Paul was a believer in teamwork. Numerous places in his writings it came through, but perhaps nowhere as evident as 1 Thessalonians 5:11 where he said, "So encourage each other to build each other up, just as you are already doing" (TLB).

OK, Dad, modeler, encourager, teacher, player/coach—don't miss a golden opportunity to pull your team closer together when you publicly (in front of your family) declare your support and love for your sweetheart, your wife.

4
Don't Fence Me In

There are lessons in all of life. Recently, some new insights in child-rearing have come to mind.

Two things LaVon has always wanted in a house have been:

1. for it to be ivy-covered, and
2. to have a picket fence.

The home we now have already had quite a bit of ivy growing on the brick near the front door, so all she lacked was a picket fence. I had been considering putting one up for several weeks, and finally decided to get with it. LaVon explained what she wanted: "Just a few feet of fence right here and a few more feet right over here. I don't want length, just 'effect.' "

Being the "dutiful" husband I am, I began the process of building our cute little picket fence, "not for length, but effect."

In all the marking, cutting, sealing, painting, hammering, digging, and concreting that followed, I began to see a change come over LaVon. Instead of the look of joy I had anticipated, I found instead one of puzzlement. Finally, she and Katy broke the news after I had completed about twenty feet of fence in front and twelve feet in the patio area out back. They had decided there wasn't enough " effect"—the "effect" needed to be longer. I had now completed twelve more feet of "effect"/fence in front and twelve more feet of "effect"/fence in the patio area. Instead of thirty feet of "effect," we now had well over fifty feet of "effect."

Fences make several "statements"—depending on the type of fence:

(1) "Effect" fence—decoration only.
(2) High board fence—a confusing statement of either, "We want what's inside this fence to stay inside this fence," or, "Keep out!"
(3) High cyclone fence—"I dare you to climb over this one. You can see what's here, but don't touch."

Now, what does all this have to do with rearing children? Everything. The difference is that in "raising" children, the process is reversed. The "fences/rules" go up early in the child's life, and during that child's lifetime, we should be tearing down fence—a little at a time—so that when the child is in midteen years, the fence that remains is for "effect." Problems arise because of our own interpretation of the purpose of the "fences/rules." If we build these fences and interpret them to our children to be for the purpose of "controlling" them or to "keep them in line," then the "fence" may also become a barrier between us and them. On the other hand, if our fences are low ones that allow some breathing room and freedom of vision and movement, the "effect" will allow that child to make some decisions on his or her own. Some will be good decisions, some not so good, but the child is learning, and you are there to help and encourage, rather than to control.

During the child's lifetime we as dads should, every once in awhile, tear down a "section of fence"—to allow for more freedom, responsibility, and possibility for that child to make decisions on his or her own. We begin by surrounding that newborn infant with "fence" for protection and care. Yet, when they are learning to crawl, walk, and talk, some "fence" needs to come down. The process has now begun that will continue throughout your child's lifetime until finally, in later teenage years, there remain only a few pickets for "effect."

Then comes the day when even those pickets can be torn down. Hopefully, through careful fence-removal techniques, we will be sending that child into the world with purpose in his/her life. Begin thinking through what that purpose will be. How and for what purpose will each of your children be released? Where is our example? "For God so loved the world, that he gave [sent] his only begotten Son . . ." (John 3:16, KJV). Sound familiar? Our children will not be able to accomplish what Jesus did, but the principle is still there: to release that child (without fence) so the child can now introduce others to Christ.

Think through this with me. God sent His only Son into a world knowing that the world would be hostile toward Him and finally crucify Him. I couldn't do that with any of my three children, but I could through fence removal and training equip them to enter the world with a purpose in mind—to introduce others to that Person who, centuries ago, died so they could have eternal life.

My "for-effect" fence will always be a reminder to me of the principle of raising children . . . but I have a feeling I will probably be adding more "effect" to this one—not tearing it down.

5
The Greater Kellyville
Tournament

It's official! My family members are now considered residents of Arlington. After nine months of commuting to Oklahoma on weekends, we have been reunited and are living in Arlington. Wallpaper is going up (on Saturdays and late at night); we are painting, doing yard work and handling the usual electrical and plumbing problems that come with an older home—but, the coffeepot is usually going, or some iced tea is ready, if you want to drop by.

LaVon, Katy, and I made the move (our boys will stay in Oklahoma until school is out). It's always more difficult on the wife and children than the husband. He is going into a ready-made place at his work while his wife and children are thrust into new, totally foreign territory. The spouse looks for shopping and doctors, and the child gets to be the "new kid" at school. Even our dog is getting accustomed to her new turf.

One of the things I'm trying to find for Katy is a girls' softball program. Let me tell you about her first softball experience last year and how it leads into the point I want to drive home.

Last spring, Katy was asked to play on an "Eight and Under," coach-pitch, girls' softball team. She was thrilled. I thought it would be a good experience for her—until I talked with her coach about the schedule. I found out after almost two weeks of practice that they would probably play about thirty games. It turned out to be more than that! The three months of Katy's season, however, turned out to be one of those "serendipities" that caught our entire family by surprise. (LaVon and I felt that after spending most of our boys' lives on bleachers, watching them participate in everything imaginable, it was time to watch our daughter in ballet or something similar—no way!)

Our sons and their dates spent many evenings with LaVon and me, watching Katy—shirttail out, softball cap turned backwards on her head, chewing bubble gum—knocking the cover off the ball. Her team ended their season with a 34-4 record, won their league, and then beat the all-star team! Katy had a tremendous season, complete with several trophies that made her brothers green with envy. The improvement in the girls was unbelievable; their coach was a veritable "Pied Piper." LaVon and I had not expected to become as caught up in the games as we did. In fact, we were dreading it at first.

The season began with a tournament—the "Greater" Kellyville Tournament I have named it—about thirty minutes out of Tulsa in a small town with one store and service station combined. (As a friend I grew up with used to say, "It was so far out in the country, they had to have 'piped-in' sunlight.") The softball fields were really bad; and in the first game of the tournament on Friday night, our girls were beaten badly. LaVon and I commented to each other, "It's going to be a long season."

However, Saturday was a new day, and our girls looked like an entirely different team. They began their first game at the bottom of the "losers" bracket and began their climb out of the cellar. There was a concessions stand; that day, my diet consisted of five cups of coffee, two hot dogs, and a package of corn nuts. LaVon and I watched in slack-jawed amazement as these "giant killers" climbed, climbed, climbed. They had begun play at 8:30 AM, and by 5:30 PM had played and won five consecutive games! Then they played in the championship game against the team that had beaten them the previous night. Our girls not only beat them —they won big! They received individual trophies about two feet tall (almost as tall as some of the girls); and even though they were exhausted, their season was off to a 6-1 start. They had tasted victory and success. They learned not to give up, and their self-esteem was raised by quantum leaps!

Contrast this, if you will, with another scene I have reenvisioned a hundred times that took place in that same tournament. It still sends cold chills . . .

Early on Saturday morning, I had been watching a young mother (not with our team) who was having an unusually difficult time handling her children whose ages were probably three, eight, and ten. Finally, in frustration, she slapped the little boy (eight years old) and then, at the top of her lungs, reamed him out with a bleacher-filled, wide-eyed audience watching and listening—calling him, among other things, "fat," "stupid," and "lazy" (she also called him several things I can't mention here). I've contrasted the effects of that day on the self-esteem of that little boy and on those girls on Katy's team. I watched that little boy with big tears in his eyes, completely humiliated and defeated, turn from his mother and walk slowly away. Who can measure the effects of that day on the future of that young boy?

Dad, what happens to the extremely fragile self-esteem of the child/children in your home? Think back on the past few days and your communication with your children. Do your conversations revolve around what they are *not* doing right? Is there some praise? How do your children see you—nagger, complainer, impossible to please—or, as a source of affirmation, encouragement, and understanding? If you were suddenly removed from your family by death, how would your children remember you? Is there more to remember you by than someone who wanted their child's room picked up, garbage carried out, lawn mowed, good grades, and perfect friends?

This has stuck with me: a friend of mine once told me that, no matter what happened in any given day at his work or at home, his daughter would know of his love for her before she retired for the night.

Balance and attitude are the key words. There must be a certain amount of discipline and building of responsibility into our children—but without ridicule, humiliation, and physical abuse. The other side of the scale is: the balance must carry with it love, respect, encouragement, and trust. Is your child involved in some activities that will build self-esteem?

Maybe, Dad, just maybe, after you think carefully over your relationship with your children, you'll discover that it's time to go into the "construction" business—constructing a positive, healthy self-esteem for and with your children. Begin with the foundation—*your* attitude and *your* determination to put the right materials into the construction.

To paraphrase the Scripture, "Don't let the sun set on your anger" (see Eph. 4:26). Don't let the sun set on your frustration with your children, with your attitude bent all out of shape, with resentment toward them. Talk it over calmly. You know, sometimes apologies are even in order—apologies from dads.

Most of us have been known to "blow it" royally here and there.

6
A New Semester

A thought when the New Year arrives: A brand-new year with new hopes, new resolutions—a time of "new beginnings," another "Genesis" for all of us. We sort of shed the old year like a cocoon and get ready for the new. What are your hopes, your resolutions for your family this next year?

We are beginning a new "semester" in our lives, and whether any of us realize it, we subconsciously "grade" ourselves on the semester just past and anticipate what the new holds in store. We all operate throughout life on the "semester principle." How did you grade yourself on your family life last semester? Why don't you try to bring up your grade point average (GPA) next semester?

Let me suggest that you begin by calendaring into each week time with your wife and your children. A study was made in recent years of three-hundred seventh- and eighth-grade boys to see how much time their fathers spent communicating with them alone. The study ran for two weeks; at the conclusion of those two weeks, it was found that the fathers had spent an average of seven-and-a-half minutes each week with their sons! Then we are so surprised when these same boys don't "turn out" like we had planned. How much time do you spend with your children?

The same principle also applies to your marriage. Let me briefly relate the story of a good friend. I can do this because this friend gave his (and his wife's) story to a Tulsa newspaper and asked them to run the story so others could learn from their mistakes!

If anyone ever lived under a rainbow, it was Steve Davis. Steve grew up in a small Eastern Oklahoma town. He was an outstanding Christian young man, ordained to the ministry, an unusually talented football player, and a gifted student.

Steve was heavily recruited as a high school senior to the University of Oklahoma—almost every young boy's dream in that state. At O.U., Steve played quarterback for three years. Their record those three years was 32-1-1, and they won two national championships. It appeared Steve was "Destiny's Darling," with constant demands during that time and since—jetting coast to coast with speaking engagements, courted as a candidate for Congress, doing "color" for nationally-televised college football games, and founding two businesses.

Amid that whirlwind was his family. Judy was a beautiful, talented Christian lady who was very much in love with her husband. Bo was an energetic four-year-old little guy who worshiped his father. So, what could possibly be the problem at Camelot? Steve and Judy filed for divorce Monday, December 23, 1985. They had it all, and yet they had nothing. Steve and I had many long talks about this some years ago. He admitted at that time he knew his priorities were confused and that he "had to get off the treadmill." In the interview with the reporter, his words were, "I became a young man in a hurry, who got on a treadmill and couldn't get off. I did not make Judy a priority. It became a lonely life for her. When Judy told me two weeks ago that she wanted a divorce, she said, 'Steve, I'm not divorcing you; I am divorcing the situation.' "

You see, Steve's eighty-hour work week and drive for success had devastated his family. He led an exciting life, but it was void of lasting substance. In his own words from the interview, "I enjoy my involvement in college football television, and it is financially rewarding, but it has taken a terrific toll. I have paid the price. Bo is precious to me. I may have realized too late that I didn't make Judy a priority, but my son is a priority."

I know how much Judy and Bo mean to Steve, but a family can only catch the leftovers for so long. No family can exist forever on table scraps.

I urge you to make a resolution that this new semester will be the Year of the Family. For, whatever your priorities might be at this time, learn from an All-American, Steve Davis—"Stop, look, and listen"—for your family's sake.

Hug your kids and wife today, and hold on for dear life!

7

My Family . . . A Heart Transplant

I'd like to ramble a bit. I have probably assumed a lot since you are probably not aware of my family's "living arrangement," or about my family in general.

First, how about "Heart Day" (Valentine's Day)? How is it observed in your home—or is it observed at all? "Oh oh"—some of you guys are already in trouble. If you haven't caught on yet, Heart Day (really any day) could be your golden opportunity really to "rack up the points" with your wife! Of all days in the year, this is one for you to be creative—do something out of character for you. You know, be romantic! How about flowers, dinner at her favorite restaurant, a love letter like you wrote *before* you were married, a night away for the two of you in some out-of-the-way place? I also repeat: —this is the best of all gifts you can give your children— to show them how much you love your wife, their mom.

Several years ago, after LaVon and I had led a marriage-enrichment retreat, a lady sent me a copy of this poem her husband had written to their infant daughter.

> J'Nae, you're just a few days old
> But somehow I can tell;
> In all my dreams of love and life
> You'll fit in very well.

Sometimes I stare for hours on end
To glimpse each wink or nod;
And as I watch, I smile and think,
"Who says there's not a God?"

I'd like to give you some small gift
To show how much I care.
The kind of gift you'll always have
No matter when or where.

I thought of gold, of diamonds bright
Or flowers for your hair.
Of cars, or clothes, or bank accounts
To show how much I care.

But one gift always comes to mind
Much more than any other.
And so, this gift I give to you:
"J'Nae, . . . I love your mother."

Now, a little about my all-time favorite topic—my family. Just to give you a thumbnail sketch, there are five of us—six including our three-year-old Yorkshire terrier, "Pudding":

LaVon and I have been married twenty-two years. She is an "avid" antiquer, home-decorator deluxe, arts and crafts lover and creator, fantastic Sunday School teacher, can shop nonstop for six days but gets winded walking around the block, loves to entertain in our home, meticulous housekeeper, very organized, super mom, and a fantastic wife.

Jarrod is a nineteen-year-old college freshman at Tulsa University, very intelligent with a wide range of interests, engulfed in athletics, and a dedicated Christian.

Josh is a seventeen-year-old high school senior. He had a great football season (made honorable mention All-State), has a great sense of humor, is a good student who loves the Lord.

"Katy"—Molly Kathryn—is eight years old, a bright second grader who loves softball, riding her bike, "Pudding," and "wrapping her daddy around her little finger." She adores her big brothers.

Me—I love sports, antiquing, people, my work, my family, and the Lord.

Those folks have been the best teachers I have ever had. They constantly teach me lessons about life, priorities, loving, giving, and faith.

When I first moved to my present position, for many months I was with the family about forty-eight hours a week. That was all—we learned to make the most of the time we were together. We had to plan it out. We learned how precious time is and how much we had taken it for granted. Each period with them was and is like a "heart transplant." I've found anew how family relationships are only temporary. A few hints on how to make the temporary time more productive and meaningful:

> . . . time together
> . . . observe
> . . . listen
> . . . play
> . . . talk

. . . laugh
. . . cry
. . . pray,
. . . celebrate

with these people called "family." A book from a few years ago was entitled *Celebrate the Temporary*—appropriate. God gave us families for a purpose. If you haven't yet discovered that purpose, make February, and every other month, your "Christopher Columbus" month!

(Written for Valentine's Day)

8
Kids Versus Lawns

Spring always reminds me of so much. As I write this it's just around the corner. If I imagine really hard, I can almost smell the linseed oil I used to rub my ball glove with every year, or I can hear the crack of the *wooden* bat against the ball. And I can vividly smell wintergreen from the dressing room in track for all of my junior high, high school, and into the college years. I can remember the "butterflies" before a race, the bang of the gun, and that satisfying sound of spikes digging into cinders. (Do the cinders date me?)

I remember what I learned about life through running, the discipline, and merely observing people. In baseball, it was the same—to try and work it into my schedule so I could play in the summer leagues.

There is one springtime lesson I will never forget. It was taught me over a decade ago.

We had recently moved to Houston. The boys were in grade school. We were moving to Houston from Abilene where we had lived for six years, and where the boys had done all of their real "memory-building" growing up. Those had been terrific years for the boys. Now, all of a sudden, we were transplanted to the hustle and bustle of Houston. It was a shock to all of our systems. We had gone through the summer months with the boys making a couple of friends in our neighborhood, but they missed their old neighborhood in Abilene where there were seven boys within a half block of each other, and within a two-year age span. Those boys had been inseparable.

Finally school began, and the boys started to make a few friends. A few weeks into school, I came home one day and there were *seventeen* kids in our front yard! I didn't even know we could stand seventeen kids upright in our yard at one time because it was so small— but I counted 'em! They were playing football, and I was thrilled at the sight! The next day there were *more* kids, and I noticed that some of my grass was being torn up. We had a few rain showers the next couple of days, but those kids still played football every day—and my yard was being demolished.

Finally, on the fifth day when I drove in and saw all of this "craziness" I stormed into the house! I let LaVon have it about *my* lawn (and she hadn't even played one bit of football). She allowed me to rant and rave, leaving venom all over the house. When I finally got it all out of my system, this "sage" of a woman quietly put me in my place.

She said, "Larry, for months now, you have been concerned about the boys making friends here. They're doing that! We have talked so many times about how quiet it is without all the neighborhood gang the boys had before. Do you hear those 'happy' sounds out there? And last, and surely least of all, is your precious grass. (This was the zinger—the creme de la creme.) You can always replant grass, and there will always be time for a lawn, but, you don't get 'overs' on the boys, and we won't always have them!" And you know, she was right on both counts.

I "sprigged" the yard and the next spring had a beautiful lawn. I never did win the "Lawn of the Month" in our subdivision, but no big deal.

In just a couple of months, the boys will both be "gone." Jarrod is already in college, and Josh will be off to college next fall—for all practical purposes—"gone."

It doesn't seem possible that all of this happened several years ago. The boys have done so much growing up, and I've seen some lawns come and go, but lawns don't seem so important to me anymore.

So, every spring, I think back on the "resurrection" of our Houston lawn and how the first part of LaVon's prophecy came true.

This spring, however, I'm seeing the second part of her prophecy come true. That's the prophecy I've dreaded seeing fulfilled.

God gives us these "gifts" called children and expects them to be high on our priority list—higher than our work, our golf game, television, ball games, naps, and even lawns.

Spring is renewal, reawakening, and resurrection time for nature. Isn't it just like God to plan it that way? Why not renew my "springtime" lesson with me this year and move your children up a few rungs on your "priority" ladder?

9
A "Worm's-eye" View
of Central Expressway

Spring break is that splendid time of the year when those in the teaching profession have a brief respite, and parents have the opportunity of going into "Spring Training" for a week so they won't forget that summer vacation is not far away.

One particular spring break had taken on a new look for us with Jarrod and Josh both on break one week, and Katy the next. Then we were at the midpoint of the boys' break from college, and it had already been an eventful learning time for us all. It began on Saturday night. Jarrod and Josh had gone to the Tulsa, Oklahoma, area for a couple of days before starting home, and they were driving their own cars to Arlington. About 10:30 Saturday night, Josh called from Sherman, Texas, to tell us his car had broken down. He had made it to a parking lot at a hotel. We asked him to leave it and promised we would go back Monday and try to have it fixed. They came home that night, and we were up well past 1:00 AM talking and watching them eat.

Sunday was an superb day at church. Since Saturday had been Josh's nineteenth birthday, we celebrated that on Sunday. Looking back, I now know that God gave me Sunday to prepare me for Monday.

Bright and early Monday morning, Josh and I headed
for Sherman. I took every tool I owned (screwdriver
and pliers) along just in case. I also had jumper cables
and a tow chain. When we reached Josh's car, we
managed to start it in just a few minutes, received di-
rections to "Flash's Auto Repair Shop," and all was looking good. I guess it was "Flash" himself who examined
Josh's car. After about thirty minutes, he located our
problem (he thought). Two crossed wires had caused a
drain on the battery (Josh had it put in only three days
earlier), and Flash said we would have to replace it, but
that we should be able to make it home.

We were ready to start back to Arlington. Everything
was going smoothly. I was ahead of Josh as we began to
move into some heavier traffic when we were coming
into Dallas. In a little while, though, the traffic began to
slow down to a standstill. I looked back and Josh was still
there. The next time I looked back, he was several car
lengths behind me—*and not moving!* I looked at my
watch and realized it was exactly 12:00 noon, Central
Expressway in Dallas, and we were in the left lane,
literally bumper-to-bumper traffic. What would I do
now? I had several options:

(1)   Leave him and pretend I didn't know who he
       was,
(2)   Try to exit as soon as possible and call a wrecker,
       or
(3)   Try to reach him and help him.

It didn't take long to determine that I needed to try
to reach him. I can now empathize with a salmon swimming upstream. I carefully backed my little green Hon-

da, against the traffic, to get back to Josh. Now came the real dilemma: Josh's car had a rear engine, so how would I get behind his car to try to jump it? Keep in mind that we now had Central Expressway inbound, noon traffic down to one lane. After a few minutes of "bluffing" drivers, I managed to pull behind Josh so we could jump start his car. But, as our situation that day would have it, it wouldn't start. A wrecker driver pulling another car came by and, grinning from ear-to-ear, hollered, "I'll be right back!" His smile was the only one I had seen so far. We had seen many faces, none of them smiling.

Now we were facing dilemma number two. I needed to maneuver back into the single lane of traffic, go in front of Josh so I could hook up the chain to tow him out of his predicament. After a few minutes, I was able to make it back in front of him. Now, get this picture: I was flat on my back under his car, trying desperately to find someplace to hook the tow chain amid all that plastic! As I listened to the honking and watched from under his car the legions of cars coming and going in every direction, my life began to flash before me and I thought, *Is this what it has all boiled down to—dying under this car on the Central Expressway?* Then it hit me, *This is going to be one of those experiences I'll be able to look back on for a long time. Some day, I'll be able to laugh about it.* All of a sudden, I remembered one of my "standby" verses in Ephesians 5:15-16 which simply says, ". . . making the most of every opportunity" (NIV)

As I kept working with the chain, I thought back on the day and realized that Josh and I had already spent some quality time together as we drove to Sherman. It

had given me an opportunity to catch up on what was
happening in his life—friends, school, fraternity, plans
for future, church, and the like. It had been a good
time, and with that thought I began to relax a little
more. In a few minutes, with great finesse, we left the
traffic, and I towed him into an auto-repair shop where
we awaited the verdict. It was going to be awhile, so we
grabbed a burger, and in our conversation, Josh introduced me to "The Student's Prayer":

Now I lay me down to rest,
A stack of books upon my chest.
If I should die before I wake,
    That's one less test I'll have to take.

We were able to visit some more while we waited for
the car to be repaired. Finally, and with some hesi-
tance, we once again started for Arlington. We made it
in by midafternoon.

That spring break went well since then. Our family
met some friends that evening and went to see one of
the best family movies we had seen in a long time—
Hoosiers. It was a great way to end the day! We then
went home, and LaVon, Jarrod, Josh, and I stayed up
late playing games.

The next Tuesday, Jarrod and Josh had lunch with
their little sister at her school—talk about a little girl
walking tall! Katy was the celebrity of her third-grade
class.

Then, one of Josh's fraternity brothers flew in to
spend the rest of the week, so, the three boys have gone
to watch a North Texas State/Oklahoma State baseball
game.

Let's return to that verse, ". . . making the most of every opportunity." That should be a verse written on the inside of our eyelids, dads. Sometimes we become so entangled in the event/crisis that we can't see any "opportunity"—"We can't see the forest for the trees." William Blake once wrote:

> He who binds to himself a joy
> Does the winged life destroy;
> But, he who kisses the joy as it flies . . .
> Lives in eternity's sunrise.

Jesus put it a little differently, "I came that they may have life, and have it abundantly" (John 10:10, RSV).

There is joy all around us. There is humor in many situations that we see as catastrophic! There is cause for celebration in many of our everyday experiences. If we would only learn to "make the most of every opportunity . . ." with our family. If we would "[kiss] the joy as it flies" and reach out and grab the serendipities that fly in and out of our lives so quickly. If we could only learn to live the "abundant life" that Christ wants us to live—how much more relaxed we would be. We would be able to feel that "uptightness" leaving our body and mind. Life would have a lot more quality to it.

In *Hoosiers* one of the basketball players insisted on praying about everything. In one scene, during a crucial point in the game, the coach (Gene Hackman) told him to go in, and the boy dropped to his knees to pray. The game was being held up by his praying. Finally, the coach went to him and said, "God wants you in the game." There is a time for prayer and meditation and concern. And there is a time to come out of the bleachers or off the sideline and get into the game! Get into the game with your family, "make the most of every opportunity" even if it's from a worm's-eye view of that infamous Central Expressway! Amen.

10
Family Worship Experiences

If you and I truly believe what Scripture says very plainly, " Train up a child in the way he should go, and when he is old he will not depart from it" (Prov. 22:6, RSV), then we must realize the importance of consistent worship experiences at home as well as at church. Sometimes we leave the spiritual training up to church leaders: " That's why I take/send my child(ren) to church. Their Sunday School, GA, and choir leaders will teach them. Our pastor will give them everything they might need so that they will grow into strong, mature Christian adults."

Wrong! The main responsibility is in *your* corner, Dads. We are "guilty as charged" of assuming that someone else will take care of that responsibility. Where should your children learn about love, honesty, respect, integrity, responsible living, scriptural values, God's love, the teachings of Christ, the richness of the Proverbs, and the plan of salvation? *At home!* There is no richer treasure in all of life than to be a part of your child(ren)'s decision to accept Christ into their lives. (I even had the wonderful privilege of baptizing Katy.) It is our responsibility and privilege, Dads, to help our children understand the importance of a *consistent* time spent in God's Word, and a *consistent* time spent in communication with God. In order for that to happen, dads need to set the example.

If you will visit with any juvenile judge, you will find a very interesting statistic—very few Jewish young people appear before a juvenile judge. Why? Because of the teaching that takes place in Jewish homes. They take literally the teachings of their faith—that the family is more than just a group of people living under the same roof. The moral, ethical, and spiritual training is the responsibility of the father to instill in that family. Read carefully the following passage from *The Living Bible:*

> So keep these commandments carefully in mind. Tie them to your hand to remind you to obey them, and tie them to your forehead between your eyes! Teach them to your children. Talk about them when you are sitting at home, when you are out walking, at bedtime, and before breakfast! (Deut. 11:18-21)

It doesn't get much plainer than that! I didn't read any mention of leaving the teachings of our faith to a Sunday School teacher or even to the pastor.

Now, how do we go about doing this? How do I begin? Good questions. Some simple suggestions:

(1) A meaningful but brief time of prayer at each meal. Set the example.
- Perhaps at breakfast, simply find out what everyone has facing them for the day, and briefly mention those needs in prayer.
(2) A time of prayer in the evening, depending on

the age of the children, would need to take on a
different look.

- For younger children, you need to help them
  with bedtime prayers—teach them, but always
  let them verbalize their own prayer—that's vitally important.
- As the children grow older, continue to help and
  encourage them but eventually help them to establish their own "time alone with God."

(3) Family worship experiences can be very meaningful and significant but they need to be geared
toward our entire family—not just the children or
the parents. This is where we can all use some
help—resources.

- Our own church library has a number of books
  that can be very helpful.

How do you begin? Why not with a very special family worship experience next Wednesday night? We will
have no prayer service at church that night, since it is
"Family Week," so the timing would be ideal for you to
begin that evening.

Make it a special time—but fairly brief. In planning
this time together, allow opportunity for each family
member to be a part of the worship experience. You
might want to make this a commitment time to each
other and to the Lord that your family will make a
covenant to be a strong family, with God at the very
center of your home.

You could begin by reading to your family Psalm
127:3: "Children are a gift from God; they are his reward" (TLB). Explain to your children—each one—
why you love them. Explain your love for your wife.

Then, explain your love for the Lord. Finally, explain your commitment to God and to your family to begin to build an even stronger family. Ask your family to join you and to voice any feelings they might have or ideas of how to make your family stronger. After you have done this, discuss *how* you will begin to put your plan into action and when. When you feel everyone agrees on a plan, join hands and commit this plan to God, asking each person to voice even a sentence prayer affirming their own personal commitment.

The family worship experience and training that a child receives at home should be the most important and consistent exposure to Christian principles he or she receives. Supplemental reinforcement would be what a child receives at church. But church experience is vital for each child to have. They can see many, many examples there of what they are learning from Scripture. The church becomes a giant-screen visual aid for a child each Sunday, as he or she sees Christian principles reinforced through adult leadership throughout our church. Be certain that they have exposure on a consistent basis.

11
How Does Your Garden Grow?

It's "Family Month"—celebrated each year in our denomination during the month of May. Actually, one week of the month is set aside to observe as "Christian Home Week," but since we are a special church with special dads like you, we celebrate Christian homes and families the entire month.

First of all, what is a Christian home? Jay Kesler wrote a book several years ago entitled, *I Want a Home with No Problems*. Your first thought is probably, *Yes, and the theme song for the film version of the book could be "To Dream the Impossible Dream"!* Of course, no one has or could have a home void of problems. But wait a minute. Don't give up. We don't live perfect, unblemished lives as individuals either, but that doesn't stop us from taking the daily challenge from Philippians 1:6, "Being confident of this very thing, that he who began a good work in you will perfect it until the day of Jesus Christ" (ASV). He works on our families, too! The real question is, Do we continue to work with our families?

A provocative statement made several years ago by Ken Chafin still haunts me: "If the family fails, then all the other institutions of society will fail." The responsibility to be certain that that scenario doesn't take place rests squarely on your shoulders and mine. So what's a dad to do? "How can I take some positive, confident steps in the right direction to help my family to become all that God really wants it to be?" There are some obvious things we can do, and some other steps that might be somewhat obscure at first.

Gardening has a lot in common with raising children. I have very fond, warm memories of my grandparents' garden in a small north central Oklahoma town. As a little boy, I remember vividly enjoying tomatoes, corn, radishes, green onions, okra, watermelon, and a lot more wonderful delicious foods fresh from the garden. I can almost taste those juicy, plump tomatoes; and to relive a summer evening sitting on their front porch listening to "Fibber McGee and Molly," "The Green Hornet," "The Great Gildersleeve," and a host of other radio shows, while working my way through a huge slice of watermelon fresh from their garden is one of the most peaceful, worry-free memories that I can conjure up.

But there is so much more to growing a good garden than throwing out some seed, fertilizing, and sitting back to enjoy the fruits of the land. Children don't come with instructions attached with the reassuring words that they will be mature, responsible adults at twenty-one. I remember my grandfather and his plow "turning the soil." Then, with a lot of back-bending hoeing and raking, he would prepare the soil for planting. He knew how to prepare the different rows for different vegetables, how to protect the plants from disease and insects, how to fertilize, when to water, and so on. My grandfather didn't create plants or seeds, but he did cultivate the soil and create the right conditions in which growth could take place.

In many ways, Dad, you and I are like gardeners with one enormous exception—our crop is vitally more important! Sometimes we must "plow up" some of our old routines and "pull out by the roots" some elements in our lives that won't provide a good, healthy atmosphere for growth. We will have to learn more about cultivating and nurturing children—recognizing how to know what's going on underneath the soil as well as what is visibly apparent. What are some of the "predictable" stages your family will go through and how do you handle, salvage, and nurture your family in those *un*-predictable times? Become a well-read, "prepared-for-all-stages" gardener/dad.

By the way, how are the "fruits" of your "garden" maturing at this time? "How does *your* garden grow?"

12
Our Best Investments—"FNs"

"The Great Pumpkin Fight" was under way! What had begun as a quiet, carve-your-own-Halloween pumpkin night at home had now turned into the "Great Pumpkin Fight" in our backyard. Jarrod and Josh were eleven and twelve, Katy was two—never mind how old Larry and LaVon were. It was another " family night" for the Link household, but somehow this one had gotten out of hand.

The giggles, squeals, screams of laughter and everyone ducking for cover happened because I had just flipped one of the boys with one of those slippery pumpkin seeds. The next thing I knew, we were digging out handfuls of that gooey, orange, stringy mess and flinging it at each other at close range. LaVon had already run inside the house, and Katy was doing her best to get into the free-for-all. It all ended with each of us being taken down and having pumpkin smeared all over us. We literally had to be hosed down before we could go inside.

This was one of probably several hundred "Family Nights" our family has experienced over the years. We started family nights at our house in 1975, when I decided my priorities were completely out of whack, and

I had better do something to remedy that, or I would be faced with raising a houseful of strangers. We immediately set up a time each week when we could guard with our lives as a time that we could be together. That Thursday night time became as sacred to our schedule as our Sunday schedule was.

"Family Night" was a tradition from the time the boys were seven and eight, until well into their junior-high years. Since that time, we have had to revolve family nights around school activities, the boys' work schedules, and so forth. We haven't always been able to get together in recent years; but whenever it has been possible, we have celebrated a night together.

In the recent move of LaVon and Katy to Arlington, we have made this same commitment to Katy of a "Family Night" on Thursdays.

Time after time, we have all realized and verbalized the importance of these nights together. There was the time in Houston when we received a call from good friends of ours. Their marriage was in serious trouble and they wanted to know if their son could spend some time with us while they tried to get through some of their problems. During one of our family nights while he was there he told us how he wished his family would spend some time together. In talking with our boys in recent days—now eighteen and nineteen—about memories, they both have verbalized that these family nights were significant to them.

We have never had much money to invest in CDs or IRAs, but our family has had its own form of CDs—investing chunks of time into FNs (Family Nights). It continues to yield benefits.

May is Family Month for our church. During this

time—and anytime—I urge you to make time for your
family like never before. Experiment with Thursday
night, or any night, as long as you make an attempt at
a family time. Be careful, though. You might get
"hooked" on your family. I have included a few suggestions that you might use. You can do almost anything—
as long as you do it together. (We will be spending a
portion of our Thursday nights at Katy's softball games.)

The church calendar is cleared on Thursday, so that
we, as a church, can make a statement—that family life
is important. Why don't you make that same statement
to your family? I hope you will. From one father's perspective (mine) . . . "It has made all the difference in the
world. I fell in love with my family years ago, and I'm
a richer man because of it."

How Our Family Began:
Family Night #1

Either take the phone off the hook or unplug it for a
couple of hours:

(1) Explain to your children ahead of time that you
     will be discussing how your family began.
(2) Begin your evening with a light dinner that can
     be cleared and cleaned quickly.
(3) During your mealtime prayer, commit that
     evening to God, thanking Him for your family.
     (Call each family member by name during your
     prayer.)
(4) Be certain that each person helps in clearing the
     table after dinner.
(5) Find the most comfortable spot in your house, or

perhaps in the backyard on a blanket on the ground.

(6) You might start by talking about your parents (your child[ren]'s grandparents), and back another generation or two if you can. Tell them some history about their ancestors.

Talk with them about your own childhood—some funny things that you did, or that their grandparents did. Tell them how it was for you growing up. (Don't get " bogged down" in when-I-was-your-age, I-walked-sixteen-miles-to-school-in-snowstorms-uphill-and-down stories. They're boring!) Keep this time light and humorous. For example, "The day before our class pictures were made when I was in the first grade, I collided on the playground at school with another boy. On picture day, I had *two* black eyes." (True story)

Talk with your children about your dating and courtship days, your wedding, their birth (the excitement and adjustments of those times). Talk with them about when they were infants and bring them up to the present.

Turn the tables on them and ask them to tell you about some of their earliest memories—" What do you remember the most about when you were very young?"

Remember that the goals for tonight are:

(1) To learn about family;
(2) To keep it "light" if possible (work for smiles and giggles); and
(3) To finish the evening with a stronger sense of family heritage.

Don't be threatened by questions! Answer them as
directly as possible. Nothing will bring your family
together more quickly and in stronger fashion than for
your children to feel that they will get *legitimate* an-
swers to questions they have.

- Don't make the evening a lecture when just parents talk. Allow time while you're talking for your
  children to comment or question.
- Take your time with the evening. Don't try to rush
  through it!
- Close your time together with a prayer of thanks
  for your family. Ask each member to thank God for
  the person on his or her right.

Game Night:
Family Night #2

"Game Night" has always been one of our favorites.
We usually take turns selecting games; and if they are
longer games (lasting many hours), we play a time limit.
(By the way, we have learned that LaVon always cheats
at Monopoly. We can never allow her to be the banker.)

We always have snacks (popcorn, cookies, nachos, or
ice cream) on hand before we begin. Some of our favorite games have been Rook, Wahoo, Monopoly, Go to
Texas, Charades, and The Ungame. We have learned a
lot about each other in these games, and we have broken down many barriers at the same time.

First of all, set a time limit for the evening. Then, let
your children select a game or two. You might want to
try to teach them a new game. If you just can't "get
into" the game, an alternative would be to pull out a

puzzle that the whole family can work on at the same time.

Make sure you have a break at some time during the evening for snacks. Let the kids help prepare it.

The "Ungame" is a communications game that is excellent to use to get an inside look at your children. There are no winners or losers. Its sole purpose is to encourage you to answer "What if . . ." type questions, or you may ask questions of the other players.

Usually the faster the game moves, the more enjoyable it is for the children, so plan accordingly.

Close your time together with a prayer of thanksgiving for a time to play together.

Picnic:
Family Night #3

What child doesn't like a picnic? What adult, who will allow himself to be a child for a while, doesn't like a picnic?

This night doesn't have to be in a park, even though your family may prefer that. Food is important, but the *fun* of the picnic is the most important. You may decide you want to have a wiener roast or charcoal hamburgers, or you might stop by and pick up something on your way to the picnic spot. Just make sure your time there isn't all spent in preparing and eating the food.

Become a child. Don't take lawn chairs to sit and watch your children. *Play* with them. Go for a nature walk, "explore" with them, play catch with a ball, play soccer, swing on swings, or go down the sliding board with them. Your children need to know that it's OK for adults to play at times. If they don't see that, they will dread adulthood because "you can no longer have fun."

Make certain that everyone is tired; but before you leave your picnic spot, find a place (maybe in your car) that you can all stop and thank God for the fun that you've had together.

Television or Movie Night: Family Night #4

Thursday night is a great night for this! Television is probably at its best for early evening viewing; and you won't have to wait in line if you decide to go out to a movie. This night presents a lot of possibilities, but you need to plan ahead.

(1) If there is a suitable movie on at a theater and you can somehow grab a sandwich, then you can make it to an early movie and (a) get in cheaper, and (b) be out of the theater in time so that your children won't have to be up late.

(2) Of course, it's hard to beat the TV lineup on Thursday night with family-oriented shows like "The Cosby Show" and "Family Ties." (These shows are both loaded with great springboards for discussion with your kids.)

(3) If you have a VCR and can rent a family favorite, that opens up another possibility.

Two things to work for on this night:

(1) A time to all eat together, if possible, and

(2) A time to talk about what you have watched.

As always, close your evening with a prayer of thanksgiving for the time together and for whatever discussion that may have resulted.

Cooking and Commitment Night: Family Night #5

Plan a meal that everyone likes and that everyone can help to prepare. Make it a special night with your finest dishes, silver, candles. You might even eat in the dining room. (By the way, it's OK to have pizza served on fine china, if that's what your family wants.) Be certain that *everyone* has a part in the preparation or the cleaning—maybe both. Also, be certain that there will be no interruptions—phone unplugged, television off and so forth.

Enjoy a leisurely meal complete with bragging on, "How well Mike set the table," or "What a great job Mandy did in grating the cheese," and so forth. After you have finished the meal, clear the table, clean the kitchen, and regroup in your most comfortable spot, on the floor, in a circle, close together.

Beginning with one of the parents, tell what you have enjoyed the most about the family nights. Then, ask each person to do the same. If you are willing to follow through, you might then ask if your family would like to continue to do this. If everyone is in agreement to make family night each week a very important night, then ask them to join you in a prayer of commitment:

(1) Thanking God for these five nights together,
(2) Thanking God for each family member—by name,

(3) Asking God's help in making your family what He wants it to be, and

(4) Committing these family nights not only to grow closer to each other, but closer to Him as well.

13
Father's Day or Kids' Day?

In 1976 we had a memorable summer just like many other folks. That year, LaVon wanted to go to Williamsburg, Virginia, for our vacation. I felt that the entire continent was probably going to tilt in that direction because everyone would be headed toward the East Coast to celebrate the Bicentennial. So, we compromised and went as far as Gatlinburg, Tennessee, and the Great Smoky mountains for what was probably the best vacation trip ever!

Each family member had his/her Bicentennial project. Mine was to grow a beard, which except for about three weeks in 1978 has stayed intact, although it has changed color! We were determined that there would be something in this trip for everyone, so it included our first-ever trip down a water slide, "Opryland," a ride on a tram in the Smokys, "Silver Dollar City," and more antique shops than anyone could count. Every time the boys would see an antique shop, there was "weeping and wailing and gnashing of teeth" from the backseat. It was a gleeful trip, and I received on that trip affirmation as a father that Jarrod has long since forgotten but I never will.

LaVon and I had worked diligently to be certain that

the trip would be fun for Jarrod and Josh, as well as us.
(This was BK—before Katy.) We had enjoyed not only
the sights and the adventure of the trip, but we had
prepared lists of "road games," and had played them
all—several times. It was somewhere in West Tennessee on our trip back. We were not yet to our motel stop
for the night, but just traveling along on the interstate
with the darkness pierced only by our headlights. Jarrod was leaning up with his chin rested on the seat
between LaVon and me, and we were asking some
"What if . . ." questions, when Jarrod said, "When I
grow up, I want to be a dad just like you."

It's very difficult to drive when your eyeballs are
"swimming," but that affirmation/encouragement
from my then nine-year-old son was a catalyst to me to
make me want to be more of an example to my sons
every waking minute. As we drove on through the
night, I thanked God repeatedly for the privilege of
being a father—and for giving me two sons like Jarrod
and Josh. That was just prior to Father's Day 1976.
Needless to say, that was my best Father's Day gift that
year. Now, ten years later, God has not only blessed and
strengthened the relationship of Jarrod, Josh, and me,
but has given LaVon and me another special gift—
Katy.

So, that's why I'm writing this letter with special significance from a dad who can look back on this past
decade of love, laughter, and tears—but *always* a sense
of joy and pride in my children—God's very special
blessings to LaVon and me.

To Jarrod, now nineteen
   To Josh, now eighteen

To Katy, now eight
I dedicate myself afresh and anew as a father,
and I dedicate this letter to those wonderful
"gifts" whom I have the privilege of calling
"sons and daughter."

And, all that brings me to what I wanted to write about this month.

"Father's Day," "Dad's Day," "The Old Grump's Day"—is that day celebrated, recognized, ignored, or ritualized in your home? Why is it observed like it is? Probably, the way it is observed in your home is due to the way your children are treated the other 364 days in the year.

Did you ever think about reversing the process, or giving of yourself on that day that honors you? After you have opened your tie and after-shave, why not thank your children for the privilege of being their father? Then, tell them why it's an honor to be their father—affirm them. Take this opportunity to brag about them. Tell them some of the things they do that really please you. You know as well as I do that we aren't shy about telling them what they do that we don't like. "Why don't you (a) make better grades; (b) pick up your room; (c) come home on time; (d) choose better friends; (e) turn down your stereo; (f) help around the house?" (You may choose one or all of these.)

Do you ever stop and think about what it was like when you were a boy? Personally, I'm grateful my children aren't like I was—whew! But, I don't always get that message across to them. I know a lot of the time when they have done something wrong, I can feel that metamorphosis taking place. Remember the "Incredible Hulk"? Suddenly, I change from a " man of the cloth," to this wild-eyed, ranting, and raving gargoyle, traversing my house to and fro "seeking whom I may devour." After I have completed my "fatherly" duty of letting whichever child who has crossed the "point of no return" have it with both barrels, I take a deep breath, and I feel absolutely rotten. I've done it again, and I said the last time that I wouldn't do that. What a bummer!

John Drescher wrote a book several years ago entitled, *If I Were Starting My Family Again*—an excellent outline of some things we fathers could do differently, written from the perspective of a husband/father, whose family is grown and gone. A few helpful hints from his book:

- I would love my wife more.
- I would laugh more with my children.
- I would be a better listener.
- I would try for more togetherness.
- I would do more encouraging.
- I would pay more attention to the little things.
- I would seek to share God more intimately.

He wrote about putting down the newspaper when your children talk to you and looking into their eyes— looking for the "wonderment" (my own words). It disappears all too quickly.

How about the seemingly endless questions with which parents are bombarded? It is estimated that the average child asks half-a-million questions by the age of fifteen. (For some, I believe that happens by the time they are five years old.) If you and I could only learn that we have half-a-million opportunities to share the meaning of life!

Your relationship with your child goes in cycles, just like every other relationship in life. As you and I think about that upcoming "day of days" for all of us dads, concentrate on that stage of your relationship with each of your children right after they were born, when you were wide-eyed and proud, beaming, showing pictures. What's happened? Recapture that stage—not treating them as babies, but as cherished gifts from God.

Turn the tables on them. When they ask the inevitable question heard in every household on Mother's Day and Father's Day ("When is Kids' Day?"), you can say, *"This* is your day, and I want to tell you why I'm proud to be your father!" I do want to warn you that if you follow this advice, you may get some very strange looks from your family, who is wondering as you speak, "Where are those words coming from?"

God has given us a great privilege/responsibility/ assignment/investment with those young lives entrusted to us. Are we truly deserving of the honor of a day just for us? Sometimes I question that honor in my own behalf. A haunting passage of Scripture for me begins with a familiar and often-quoted statement: "Children, obey your parents . . ." (Ever notice how the emphasis is always on *obey?*) But, continue to read in Ephesians 6:1,4—

> . . . and now a word to you parents. Don't keep on scolding and nagging your children, making them angry and resentful. Rather, bring them up with the

loving discipline the Lord himself approves, with suggestions and godly advice (TLB).

Make this "Father's Day" a special day for your entire family—do the unexpected!

14
A Time to Hug

This spring has already developed into a hectic time of balancing household schedule with both of our sons home from college for the summer. We have gone from "dainty" breakfasts and light evening meals to hired hand, nonstop "eat-a-thons" at night. LaVon, Katy, and I were buying a few things at the grocery store every two to three weeks. It was quite a shock when our bill was over $250 last week! And an even *bigger* shock when we began to run low on most things after about a week. LaVon said she really felt bad the other night when she *thought* she had cooked too much, and the boys looked at her when everything was gone as if to say, "That was a great appetizer, now where is the main course?!"

Food is just one of the adjustments to make when kids come back in from college. They have been used to college life with something happening literally twenty-four hours a day and now they're home where the most exciting thing that happens is when the doorbell rings and our Yorkshire terrier (Pudding) goes berserk, or Katy has a softball game. So, after they have been home for a few days, what happens? Not much. But you know what? It has really felt good—warm and comfortable.

We have all begun to relax and enjoy each other. Jarrod and Josh are working this summer for a company owned by one of our church members. They are selling and planting grass. Now wait a minute! I'm talking about Bermuda, Saint Augustine, and so forth. We have been able to have some good talks in the evenings when they get in from work, and one day this week was particularly good for this sentimental dad.

We didn't get through with dinner until about 7:45 and then we all gravitated to the front yard. Katy had wanted to practice her hitting for her final softball game (she has gone twenty-six for thirty at the plate including two home runs and seven triples). Jarrod and Josh were throwing passes with the football and LaVon was just walking around looking at flowerbeds and bushes. (I found out later that she was coming up with my next "project.") It felt *so* good for us to be enjoying an evening together like that.

I was reminded of the passage of Scripture in Ecclesiates 3 " . . . a time to . . . " In verse 5 in *The Living Bible* it simply says, " . . . A time to hug." I don't know the full meaning of that passage, but you know, I don't think that it has to mean a "physical" hug. It could mean "hugging that moment in time." And that's what I did the other night. Smiling to myself with a smile that went down to my toes, I "hugged that moment in time."

Later that evening, after it got so dark that:

(1) LaVon couldn't see anything else for me to do,
(2) Katy couldn't even spot the bright orange softball,
(3) Jarrod and Josh couldn't see the football,

we all crammed into my little green Honda, stopped and got a soft drink, and just drove around Arlington visiting.

It was an evening of "hugs" for all of us—not physically. We were just enjoying each other, laughing, talking, and playing together.

With everything else that's going on around you right now, find some of those "huggable" moments with your family. Then, do just that—"hug 'em tight!"

15
Summertime—Memorytime

A recent Saturday was one of those days that will be long remembered by this dad! Let me lay a little groundwork.

Some friends of ours who have a crafts business were coming to Arlington to be a part of a crafts show at the Convention Center. We invited them and their families (plural) to stay with us. Thursday night, six people pulled in to spend the night so that they could begin "setting up" on Friday morning. On Friday, a friend of our younger son, Josh, arrived to spend the weekend. On Saturday, six more people arrived including a friend of our older son, Jarrod—a total of eighteen people now at our house—six of whom are eight years old or younger! A major crisis is about to happen with that many children, so we decided we needed to "divide and conquer." We drew straws to see who got which children, and I decided to take Katy (eight years old) and Sarah (six years old) for the day. We began the day at Six Flags Over Texas here in Arlington, along with thirty thousand other people. For hours, we "had fun" standing in line for thirty minutes, riding for two minutes, standing in line for forty minutes, riding for one minute, standing in line for fifteen minutes, and watching a "pink thing" melt all over arms and legs in thirty-three seconds flat; and, to top it all off, standing in line to go to the restroom. Finally, the "fun" was over. I kept wanting to ask the girls, "Are we having fun yet?" We left Six Flags because I needed to get home to cook hamburgers for our growing crowd. (Earlier that day, I had introduced myself to a very attractive family sitting in our living room whom I had never seen before. They said they saw all the cars out front and it looked like a great party—"Just thought we would stop by for a few minutes"). There was precious little time to cook and eat because tonight was to be "Bat Night" for the Texas Rangers' baseball game. We were planning to go, and I was already worn to a frazzle!

I thought the girls would rest for a while, but they seemed to gain momentum on the way home! When we got home, several of "the younger set" went next door to swim while I cooked hamburgers.

As I sat down to eat, most of the crowd was already through and ready to go to "Bat Night." I inhaled a burger, grabbed my keys, and we were off to the game —one of those only-once-(please)-in-a-lifetime experiences. The Rangers have had very few crowds like they had that night. We arrived late enough that all the reserved seats were gone, so we sat in the right field bleachers. It was 7:00 PM, ninety-four degrees, thirty-eight thousand fans (at least thirty-seven thousand of them had bats), and we sat directly in front of about a dozen "yuppies" whose purpose in coming to the game was twofold: (1) to consume as much to drink as anyone who has ever attended a ball game of any type anywhere, and (2) to get the "wave" started. They began by buying bats from all the kids sitting around them, and then they began pounding their bats and yelling at the top of their lungs. (One of them particularly reminded me of my D.I. in basic training.) This went on for seven relentless innings! Finally, either the concessionaires ran out of "liquid refreshment" or they gave up on the wave; but, our yuppie friends left at the end of the seventh. When they did, our section sent up a mighty cheer!

So, there I sat, reflecting on the day—the hours spent at "Six Lines," that should be "Six Flags," cooking, swimming, and "Bat Night," where there was more noise from the pounding bats than in any four battles from World War II.

By now, it had cooled down to only eighty-nine, and was somewhat quieter in the final inning. Katy was sitting beside me, grinning from ear to ear, clutching ever-so-tightly in one hand her bat (made in Taiwan), in the other hand a Ranger pennant, and watching with great eagerness her hero, Pete Incaviglia ("Ink Man").

Was it worth it on this Saturday for her, and for all these folks sharing our home for the weekend? You bet! I began thinking about the Father's Day "letter" I got from Katy:

" . . . Both parents are important. Dads are the roller coaster people and moms are the cookie people . . ."

Dads ride roller coasters and moms always have freshly-baked cookies ready. I can handle that. In fact, it's pretty insightful for an eight-year-old to word it that way. Today had definitely been a "roller-coaster" day; and after all, here I was, after an all-day entertainment marathon, sitting in the right field bleachers "fully clothed and in my right mind." This was one of those "memory-building" time for Katy, for our family, and for those wonderful people who shared our home for a weekend. Years from now, we will look back and say, "Do you remember the time . . . ?"

It's summertime, one of the prime times of the year for memory building. What will be some of your child's memories for the summer? Get with it! P. S. I learned my lesson about "Bat Night!"

16
Hitting the Strike Zone

LaVon had gone to youth camp as a sponsor. Katy was a first-year, full-fledged camper at children's camp (she has grown up going to church camp but never before as a full-fledged "camper"). Josh was out of town for a couple of days, so Jarrod and I decided we would take in a Texas Rangers game.

We both reached home late that evening, so it was almost 8:30 by the time we got to the stadium, and the game was in the third inning with the Chicago White Sox leading 4-1. We didn't know that we had several surprises in store that night including the first "shocker" when we had started up the ramp to the cheap seats and were met by hordes of scouts—not baseball—"boy" and "cub" types. It was "scout night" and the grandstand sections were literally packed. By the way, I have a new picture of optimism. As we were looking for seats, I spotted a young cub scout sitting about forty rows up in dead-away center field wearing his baseball glove, ready to catch all those balls that he *knew* would be hit to him!

Jarrod and I found our seats and yawned our way through the next five innings. The ninth inning was our "shocker." I had already suggested that we leave, but

Jarrod kept saying, "I want to stay 'til it's over." So there we sat. The score was 7-2 with Chicago the apparent winner, going into the bottom of the ninth. I turned to Jarrod, and with tongue in cheek said, "Well, all we need is six runs to win this one." Chicago literally used five pitchers in the bottom of the ninth to "escape" with a 7-7 game, and to take it into extra innings. In the top of the twelfth—that's right, twelfth—the Sox got two more runs and led 9-7 going into the bottom of that inning. The Rangers began yet another rally, got the bases loaded, one out and Oddibe McDowell hit his first-ever, major-league, grand-slam home run winning it for the Rangers 11-9! The game was over at 11:45 that night. We definitely got our money's worth. Now, what are the goals for any Ranger pitcher, or any other pitcher for that matter?

(1)   For your team to score as many runs as possible?
(2)   For you to throw as few pitches as possible, and to "retire" those batters as quickly as possible?

The same goals are true for all pitchers, right? Wrong! My career as a pitcher has had the exact opposite of those goals. I have been the pitcher this spring for Katy's "coach-pitch" softball team. Coaches pitch to their own team in this league and your goals are:

(1)   To try to lob the ball into the strike zone.
(2)   Pray the girls will hit the ball so that the girls and parents won't send you "hate" mail.
(3)   To try to score the maximum allowed six runs every inning.

When the season was over, our girls (Blue Jays) went 8 and 1, which was second place in their league. They had a total of 254 runs in nine games and allowed 156 runs to be scored against them. It was quite a season as we watched our second-and-third-grade girls steadily improve through the league play. When we first began there were three girls who, when they came to the plate, I literally tried to hit their bat with the pitches. But, by the end of the season, they were all hitting well.

Katy ended the year with an .879 average. Believe it or not, that wiry little girl was one of our power hitters and known as "Slugger" on the team. She was put out at first base twice, and— "horror of horrors"—her own father struck her out twice. You have to remember in this league the object is to get the girls to hit—not to strike out. It's bad enough to strike out any of the girls, but your own daughter! Then you have to face your daughter's mother!

Let's look at this scenario and the parallels we can learn from it. The game is close and Katy comes to bat. I know without a doubt that she has the capability, on a very consistent basis, to knock the cover off the ball. All I have to do is get the ball into her strike zone. She'll do the rest. The first pitch is high and she goes for it. The second pitch is low and she goes for it also. With two strikes that wonderful, nine-year-old, "apple-of-her-daddy's-eye," looks at him with the confidence that he will get the ball where it's supposed to go because he always comes through. And I'm beginning to sweat —big-time sweat.

Now I'm pitching for the Rangers all of a sudden, in an extra inning game with bases loaded and two outs. Thousands are cheering for me, but I'm scared to death. The difference is in the Rangers game I *have* to get that next batter out. Here I *have* to get Katy to hit. My arm has no feeling, but that softball feels like it weighs thirty pounds as I get ready to throw the next pitch. I throw my pitch, overcompensating for the previous two, and it drops at the plate, Katy strikes at it—she's out. I see the look of disbelief, disappointment, and disillusionment on her face as she looks at me. I hear the groans from the other parents. There's no way I'm going to look at LaVon. Thank goodness that only happened two times this year. Both times it was my fault.

Now to the point: being a dad should always be about finding and hitting the "strike zone" for each of our children. Our goal in "pitching" to them the truths, concepts, and values of life is to get the "pitches" into their own strike zone, and to pray that they will "connect." In order for them to "connect," we must spend a lot of one-on-one practice time with them so that when they get into the "real" game—all of these things will come to them naturally. But the pressure/responsibility is still on you and me, Dad, as the "pitcher" to get the ball over the plate. Many times when we think our kids "strike out" we can put the blame squarely on our own shoulders—we didn't teach them what to do when the ball finds it's way into that child's particular strike zone.

What do we do? We determine what truths, concepts, and values we want our children to receive, and then "pitch" to them over and over so that we can find and hit each child's strike zone, and so that each child, on a consistent basis can get on base. Remember, no child bats 1.000; but with Katy's .879 I'm reminded that the more consistent we are with our pitching, the more consistent they will be with their "hitting."

" Thy word have I hid in my heart that I might not sin against [God]" (Ps. 119:11 KJV).

" Play ball!"

17
Come On Out and Play

"Corkscrew! Bonzai Boggan! Shotgun Falls! Kamikaze! Raging Rapids! Hydra-Maniac! Blue Niagara! and Der Stuka!" Sound familiar? Only if you have been to the infamous "Wet 'N Wild Water Park" here in Arlington! When I was ten or eleven years old and would get to swing on a tire across a creek and turn flips into the water, or sneak in "skinny-dipping" at the pond about a mile from my house, I would never in my wildest imagination have ever dreamed of anything that would begin to approach "Wet 'N Wild"! It would have been the ultimate for this shy, blond-haired, well-tanned, barefoot boy back in the early 1950s to think anything like that could ever exist. Why, word of highways sometimes *four lanes wide* in California was just getting back to the eastern Oklahoma town where I grew up! But, just a few weeks ago, there I was, in the midst of "Wet 'N Wild," and I couldn't help but have some "flashbacks" of my sleepy summer days in Muskogee, Oklahoma, when I was about ten or eleven years old. As I compared the sights before my eyes, the best description was slack-jawed amazement!

Katy had already been to "Wet 'N Wild" a couple of times and had been asking me all summer to take her.

So on a Friday night, along with several thousand other people, we took our "Big Gulp" drink cups with coupons from a local convenience store, and made our way to yet another of Arlington's attractions that earns us the billing as the "Entertainment Capital of Texas!" Katy had a friend visiting her for a few days from out of town, and she made the trip with us.

We had no sooner walked in the park than Katy began saying something about the "Lazy River." This is a "river" that goes all the way around the park, just about three feet deep and is supposed to be relaxing. It probably is after the park closes down and you can casually float around on an inner tube. On this occasion, however, there were several hundred of us in it at the same time. I had just walked into the "river" when I was hit from behind and knocked underwater by one of the super-duper, giant tubes that had four ladies (all in their mid-forties), all of whom looked like they should have been in Thousand Oaks working out with the Dallas Cowboys at their summer training camp instead of in Arlington. But they were having a wonderful time. When I came up sputtering, they just laughed all the louder. All this time, Katy was saying, "Isn't this great, Dad!"

Well, "Wet 'N Wild" was great! (By the way, that's what we used to call Katy when she was a baby still in diapers—"Wet 'N Wild.") We rode every ride in the park several times—that is, everything except "Der Stuka!" (If you haven't been, it's the slide that is so tall that on July Fourth, people stood at the top of it and watched the Statue of Liberty celebration in New York City!) Actually, it's only seventy-six feet high, but it sure looks more than that from the ground. So, Katy, Erika, and I had gone through all the tubes, off all the water-falls, shot all the rapids. Then it was time for the "Kami-kaze Slides"—from seventy-five feet up you slide headfirst on a mat one-half inch thick down a bending, gradual sloping slide for three hundred feet. When we finally got to the top, I began looking around, trying to act nonchalant and brave. Katy was jumping up and down and kept pointing out that we could just stay up there and watch the Texas Rangers—Cleveland Indians baseball game across Interstate 30. I very unenthusiastically agreed.

We had gotten in separate lines so that we could go down at the same time; so when it was our turn, I laid down on my mat and glanced at Katy's smiling face in the chute next to me. My only thought was, "I'm sup-posed to have my forty-fourth birthday in two days, but I don't think I'll live that long!" When it was time for us to go, my mat wouldn't move, so I had to have help getting started. Once I got going, it didn't take long to get to the bottom of the slide; but, in that time, not only did my life flash before me, but I was fully convinced that I would be the first person to go airborne on the Kamikaze Slide and "bounce" to my death! As I glided out across the water at the end of the ride, I managed a feeble smile and watched Katy jumping up and down and yelling, "Let's do it again!"

"Wet 'N Wild" was fun—really. It was fun, thought-provoking, challenging, and "freeing." I realized about fifteen to twenty minutes into the "Wet 'N Wild" ex-perience that I was relaxing, laughing, shedding a lot of inhibitions and "uptightness" that keep you and me from being able to let our hair down. Transactional Analysis (TA), for all of its good and bad "press," does some very good things. One of its basic premises, of course, is that within each of us, exists "a parent," "an adult," and "a child." Much of the time the child gets no opportunity to express itself through laughter, creativity, openness to new ideas, and so forth. At "Wet 'N Wild," I had given my "child"—that shy, little tow-haired boy within—permission to come out and play. He played for several hours, and he loved it. You know what else? His daughter loved it, too—seeing her daddy having a great time.

First Corinthians 13:11 says, ". . . when I became a man, I put away childish things." It says nothing about "childlike" things—and there is a big difference. "Childlikeness" allows all of us, regardless of who we are, how big, how rough and tough, how old, how important, how successful, how wealthy—to still possess something that I hold very dear—the ability to have fun! Once in awhile, just to let that "little boy" inside me come out and play is not only great therapy, but it's always good for my family as well. A lady who was 101 years old once told me that her seventy-four-year-old son "still acts like a little boy—he has so much fun!" I know that man very well, and she's right. His grown children and grandchildren know she's right, and they love him so much because he loves life and enjoys it very much. His vocation? A Federal marshal!

How about you? When was the last time you had some unadulterated childlike fun with your kids? If it's been a while, I'll give you permission for that little boy within you to come out and play. Go ahead. Come on out and play! Have a blast! Your kids, in fact your entire family, will love it!

18
Sweaty Eyeballs

A favorite phrase of mine, whenever anyone might feel just a bit on the emotional side—a little "weepy"— is: "It kinda' makes my eyeballs sweat." Well, the "sweaty eyeballs" epidemic hit all over Arlington again just recently. Many dads, most moms, and a whole city full of kids were stricken with this plague again. It always happens in late August and early September—the first day of school! You cry because they're leaving, and they cry because they have to go! That day marks the time that parents come to the realization that Johnny or Mary is "growing up." (You must keep in the back of your mind that these "sweaty-eyeballed" parents are the very same parents who were moaning as recently as three days ago, "I can't wait for school to start. These kids are driving my nuts!") Now, through tears they are watching their offspring getting off to school, saying to themselves, "I can't believe my baby is leaving me again!" (Then, we wonder sometimes why we seem so neurotic!)

There he stands: new "school" jeans, fresh-off-the-rack-never-worn-before shirt, clean tennis shoes, hair combed, teeth brushed, lunch in hand, and freckles shining. (Take a picture. It's the last time you'll see him that way until this time next year!)

Then, there's your little girl. She looks absolutely beautiful in her new school outfit that was so carefully selected with the first day of school in mind. "Why, she really looks like an angel!" Her hair glistens, and her eyes look so bright—she can't be another year older—but, then you realize that she is! That's when you begin to "well up" inside.

It doesn't matter if it's a son or a daughter—if they are beginning kindergarten, or going off to college—it's the same. (If you're just beginning this process, I hate to be discouraging, but it really doesn't let up—the "sweaty-eyeball" epidemic hits relentlessly every year at this time.) The main thing you must realize is that you have one of the largest support groups anywhere. We're all in the same boat.

It was dragged out somewhat at our house this year. Jarrod left in mid August for McMurry College in Abilene, Texas; Josh left a few days later for Oklahoma State University in Stillwater, Oklahoma; then, Katy started third grade about a week later at Wimbish Elementary. We would just get over one leaving when we would get hit with another departure. We were reeling for several weeks. Of course, an empty bank account accompanies the emptying next. I told my barber a couple of weeks ago that I might never see him again. With two in college, it's going to be a challenge to see on what LaVon, Katy and I will be able to exist. Bill Cosby says in his book, *Fatherhood*, that he will spend about eighty-thousand dollars getting his daughter a liberal arts degree, which will qualify her to move back home after four years of college. We will put up a sign,

"Guest Room" on the boys' bedroom after they graduate.

So, what can we do for ourselves and our kids:

(1) Realize that we're all in the same boat—kids and parents alike.
(2) Realize it was all a part of God's plan when He entrusted us with each child.
(3) Pray daily for your child(ren) to be all that he or she can be in whatever school setting they find themselves.
(4) Pray daily for yourself as a parent that you can be the encouraging, supportive, affirming role model that you need to be.
(5) Then, put feet to those prayers by daily making a conscious effort to look for ways to nurture your child, ". . . in the way he should go."
(6) Become involved in school and extra-curricular activities with your child(ren) so that you can get to know their "world" at a deeper level.

You'll always experience "sweaty eyeballs" at every "home-leaving" experience. But, most of the time, the tears experienced at "home-leaving" make the "homecoming" an even richer experience.

Give them roots, give them wings, give them prayer, and give them *you!*

19
An "Oasis" Evening

This past week has been particularly memorable and meaningful to me as a father. Last Tuesday evening, LaVon had a Sunday School class meeting. She asked me what I wanted to do for dinner with Katy. I told her I had something special in mind. Katy and I were going to have our own private weiner roast and "games and laugh" night. That's exactly what we did. We got a shovel and hoe, and dug a shallow hole in our backyard. Yes, we even dug up some grass. It'll grow back next year. Then we gathered some sticks and started our fire. (Katy wanted to rub sticks together, but I insisted that matches were OK.) She got something for us to sit on so we wouldn't get wet. Then we enjoyed a weiner roast/marshmallow roast for quite awhile. We just sat and watched the fire and talked. I was reminded during that time, of times just like that with Jarrod and Josh also.

While we were sitting there, Katy said something about her Halloween costume, and I was reminded of the fun of some past Halloweens. I remember so well the year I rented a gorilla suit for three days for some parties at church; but I wore that suit almost constantly for those three days. On Halloween Day, I drove the boys to school and opened the car door for them. The look on the faces of all those wide-eyed kids in their school was something I'll never forget. The boys had a Halloween party that afternoon, and the gorilla was the special guest. It was one of those days to remember! The boys, LaVon, and I all loved it! All of a sudden, Katy jolted me back to the present when she leaned over, giggled, and kissed me—talk about a reward—talk about an incentive for more of the same!

After a while, we buried our fire, got Katy's Yorkshire terrier ("Pudding"), loaded down the car with football, soccer ball, basketball, baseball, bat, and glove, and took off for a park. We played for about an hour whatever Katy wanted to play. We ran, played soccer, football, played tag, and played on all the playground equipment. It was quite awhile after dark when we loaded up the car again and headed off to a convenience store for something to drink. When we got home, I fixed some popcorn while Katy fixed us something to drink.

That evening was an oasis for me. I needed it. It was a blood transfusion, an escape into the wonderful world of childhood. It was a "smiler," a time when I could feel great that I had let a few things go in order to spend some very valuable time with Katy.

Then, this past weekend, Jarrod and Josh were both back home at the same time, for the first time since going away to college. LaVon cooked big and the boys ate big! We enjoyed being together, and as the "next" started emptying again Sunday afternoon and Monday, I was reminded of the value of those nights like Katy and I had spent last Tuesday. The value of family times, "kid" time, fun time, serious talks, decisions, touching, hugging, releasing.

Maybe that's the hardest part—"releasing." I hugged Jarrod as he left for Abilene on Sunday. I hugged Josh as he left for Stillwater, Oklahoma, on Monday; and I held Katy closer, knowing that all too soon, I'll be "releasing" her, too.

It's God's plan: the gift of a child, nurturing that child, teaching that child, and releasing that child.

Hug your kid(s) today, and look for opportunities for "oasis"-type experiences with them. Releasing is less traumatic if you and they have those memories.

20
The Parable of the 11½ C

This story began recently on the Wednesday before Thanksgiving. All was going very well. Jarrod had gotten home fine from Abilene for the holidays, LaVon's parents and my mother had arrived from Oklahoma. All of them came Wednesday afternoon, and Josh wasn't due in from Stillwater until Wednesday night. When he arrived and started unpacking, he said, "Dad, I forgot to bring any dress shoes." Then it registered with me: *Our family is supposed to light the Advent candle in the service Sunday morning, and I don't want him doing that in his tennis shoes. Who do I know that wears an 11½ C?* I promptly put it out of my mind, concentrating on such things as enjoying having family at home, turkey and dressing, giblet gravy, cranberry salad, and pecan pie. We really got caught up in all of that during the weekend. On one or two occasions, the thought of the 11½ C surfaced, but then submerged again very quickly. After all, we had a lot of missing family time to catch up on.

We are a game-playing group, so we had marathon games of "Go-to-Texas," "Clue," and "Rook." (Jarrod, Josh, and I stayed up 'til after 1:30 one night playing Rook.) Everybody gets into the act. Then, we also strung popcorn one evening to get a head start on the Christmas tree.

LaVon's parents and my mom had to leave on Friday, so we took them through Dallas to get them back on the right highway to get home. Afterwards, we decided we should do some shopping since we have two birthdays in the next month, plus Christmas. So, we set out for "serious" shopping, and got quite a bit done, including a picture of Jarrod, Josh, and Katy with Santa! We ended Friday with a wonderful dinner in Dallas, and finally came home to begin a marathon evening of Rook and Clue. It's been the same partners always—LaVon and Jarrod against Josh and me. (Katy waited very impatiently for us to finish Rook so we could get to her game, Clue.) We played well into the night again. Then on Saturday we headed for Fort Worth to shop and back to Arlington for more shopping and a movie. Finally, after looking for cowboy boots, we dragged home and that thought from last Wednesday came screaming at me again—*Where do I get an 11½C dress shoe?* I got in touch with a friend who said the largest he had was a 10C, but I was welcome to it. At 10:30 Saturday night I went to his home to pick up some "not-large-enough-but-as-close-as-I-could-get" shoes. In the meantime, he had been on the phone to try and help, but no 11½C was to be found.

The "moment of truth" for all of this came Sunday morning when Josh announced, "I can't get my feet into these shoes," to which I promptly replied, "No choice—you have to." If you looked closely Sunday morning, you would have noticed Josh limping slightly as we came forward to light the Advent candle. You would also have noticed that he quickly removed the shoes the second we got back to our pew.

So, where is the parable in all of this? Here lies the moral to this story: Trying to force an 11½C foot into a 10C shoe—the story of the entire holiday season—forcing too much into too little time and, as I did, postponing the importance of "the event" by getting caught up in the hustle and bustle of the present. As I have reflected on the happenings of that bygone Christmas, the parallel becomes even more apparent.

There is a fine line between celebrating and truly enjoying the holidays, and hitting it so hard that "the event" gets forced into this wonderful time of the year. There was an innkeeper two thousand years ago who got caught up in the same trap in which we find ourselves. With "no-vacancy" lights flashing at the Bethlehem Inn, he had to tell Mary and Joseph, "Well, I do have a stable . . ." It's indicative of our own hearts so many times. Our lives get so crowded with good things to do that "the event" gets the leftovers, or nothing at all. The "trappings" of the holiday season are often wonderful experiences; but they may also cause us to forget priorities. Just as I postponed borrowing an 11½C for Josh and causing the resulting crowded condition, we do the same with "the event." "I'll give attention to the real meaning of Christmas tomorrow, when I have more time." Then, we realize, "It's Christmas Day, and I haven't given time to 'the event.'" It then gets forced into a very few moments on Christmas morning, when we are gathered around the tree (with the children exploding to get their hands on what Santa has brought them), and we announce, "Let's pause for a moment and realize the importance of today . . ."

"The event," the birth of our Savior, needs to be and must be woven into the holiday season. Otherwise, we will find ourselves like the innkeeper two-thousand years ago saying, "Well, I do have a stable . . . "—just leftovers.

Dad, don't wait 'til Christmas Day or even Christmas Eve to weave into this season the significance of it all—the birth of the Savior of the world! " . . . For unto *you* is born this day . . . " Personalize that message. That's the way it was intended. In the midst of all the activity of this season, pause periodically to give thanks and to celebrate with your family the significance of "the event." Don't wait 'til 10:30 on Christmas Eve and then cause an "11½C" event to be forced into a "10C" time frame.

21
A Covenant Between Dads

In the midst of the holiday season, a time of traditions, I would like to establish a tradition—a covenant with you: a letter once a month from a "novice" father to other "novices." We form a brotherhood as fellow pilgrims along the journey called fatherhood. The journey definitely has its ups and downs—just like a roller coaster. Sometimes we scream and yell from exhilaration and sometimes we just . . . scream and yell! First, you're on top of the world, then you plummet to unknown depths—the "abyss of fatherhood." We all go through those extremes and we need encouragement. That is the reason for this letter. This won't be designed to send you on a guilt trip or to be a textbook on raising children it will be to encourage you. I'll pick a topic or two that is common to all of us and write you about it once a month.

Because we are in the midst of the holiday season and because tradition is so much a part of our lives now, how about writing on "tradition!"

Traditions are "memories in the making" for your children. They give substance to families. Many times, we middle-class, rootless, antitraditional Americans lose sight of what something as simple as "hamburgers every Saturday night at our house" can mean to give roots to children—something they can nail down and count on.

Here are some that the Link household looks forward to at this season:

(1) The Christmas tree is always bought the Saturday after Thanksgiving. (Many of LaVon's friends accuse her of buying one right after Halloween.)

(2) I usually put up outdoor lights that day while LaVon begins her Christmas decorating. It takes her several days to get everything in place. Then, our house is transformed into a veritable fairyland!

(3) A tradition we started several years ago was to have a Saturday brunch just before Christmas when each family member could invite the person who had been most significant to them during that year. They know why they are invited; and as we are about to eat, we gather in a circle and have an affirmation time when these folks are told thank you for being so meaningful in our lives.

We have several other traditions:

• saving last year's Christmas tree to be this year's Yule log on Christmas Day,
• caroling parties,
• candlelight services on Christmas Eve.

But, the tradition that is the most meaningful to our whole family is "people"—having people in our home constantly to share with them the "tradition" that began all Christmas celebrations—Jesus Christ.

Don't get too busy this year to celebrate friends, family, traditions, and Christ!

Have a merry, "traditional" Christmas!